Newfoundland &
Labrador

Newfoundland & Labrador

Lawrence Jackson

Quaerite Prime Regnum Dei

Lerner Publications Company

LIBRARY OF CONGRESS
CATALOGING-IN-PUBLICATION DATA

Jackson, Lawrence.
    Newfoundland / by Lawrence Jackson.
        p. cm. — (Hello Canada)
    Includes index.
    ISBN 0–8225–2757–X (lib. bdg.)
    1. Newfoundland—Juvenile literature.
    2. Newfoundland—Geography—Juvenile literature.
    [1. Newfoundland.] I. Title. II. Series.
F1122.4.J33 1995
971.8—dc20   94–28964
                                                        CIP
                                                         AC

Manufactured in the United States of America

1 2 3 4 5 6 – JR – 00 99 98 97 96 95

Cover photograph by Betty Groskin. Background photo by R. Chen/SuperStock.

The glossary that begins on page 68 gives definitions of words shown in **bold type** in the text.

Senior Editor
Gretchen Bratvold
Editor
Karen Chernyaev
Photo Researcher
Cindy Hartmon
Designer
Steve Foley

Our thanks to Edward Kirby, Public Information Officer, Department of Industry, Trade and Technology, Government of Newfoundland and Labrador, for his help in preparing this book.

 This book is printed on acid-free, recyclable paper.

Contents

Fun Facts

🍁 The province of Newfoundland and Labrador confuses people. It includes the island of Newfoundland as well as Labrador, a larger region on the Canadian mainland.

🍁 Clarence Birdseye got his idea for packaged frozen food in 1915, while working in Labrador. There, he saw that the fish Labradorians caught while ice fishing froze immediately. Months later, when the fish were thawed and cooked, they still tasted fresh.

🍁 Newfoundland probably got its name in 1502. That year the English king Henry VII called the region "new found land," because it had just been explored for England. Sailing on the English ship was a farmer from Portugal, who may have given the Portuguese name for "farmer"—*llavrador*—to what is now Labrador.

Hi! My name is Barkley. As you read *Newfoundland & Labrador*, I will be helping you make sense of some of the maps and charts that appear in the book.

Newfoundland sticks so far out into the Atlantic Ocean that the island is nearer to Europe than to many parts of North America. Most Newfoundlanders actually live closer to Ireland, for example, than to Manitoba or to the state of Florida.

Newfoundland's Funk Island is one of the noisiest and smelliest places on earth. The island is named after an old French word for "stink." The noise and smell come from millions of screeching seabirds, who cover the ground with their odorous droppings.

Cape Spear, on the island of Newfoundland, is the easternmost point of the province.

The rocky cliffs of the island's coast help give Newfoundland and Labrador its nickname— the Rock.

The Rock

Newfoundlanders and Labradorians fondly call their province the Rock, and most of it is. They use the nickname to joke about their struggle to make a living from this difficult place. During several ice ages that occurred long before the first humans arrived, thick sheets of ice called **glaciers** bulldozed much of the area's soil into the sea. The glaciers left part of the land covered with hard rock and soil that is generally too poor to farm.

The easternmost province of the Dominion of Canada, Newfoundland and Labrador is roughly the same size as Sweden. The province, one of the four Atlantic Provinces, borders the Atlantic Ocean. The ocean and the Labrador Sea form Labrador's eastern border. North of Labrador, across the Hudson Strait, lies Nunavut, Canada's newest territory.

A narrow waterway called the Strait of Belle Isle flows between Labrador and the island of Newfoundland. The island partially blocks the Gulf of Saint Lawrence. This body of water separates Newfoundland from New Brunswick, Prince Edward Island, and Nova Scotia—the other Atlantic Provinces.

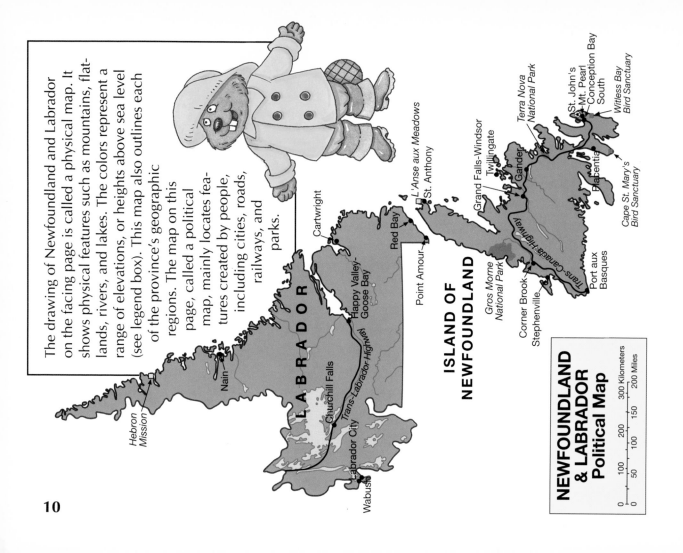

The drawing of Newfoundland and Labrador on the facing page is called a physical map. It shows physical features such as mountains, flatlands, rivers, and lakes. The colors represent a range of elevations, or heights above sea level (see legend box). This map also outlines each of the province's geographic regions. The map on this page, called a political map, mainly locates features created by people, including cities, roads, railways, and parks.

L A B R A D O R

Hebron Mission

Nain

Churchill Falls

Labrador City

Wabush

Trans-Labrador Highway

Happy Valley-Goose Bay

Cartwright

Red Bay

Point Amour

L'Anse aux Meadows

St. Anthony

Gros Morne National Park

Corner Brook

Stephenville

Port aux Basques

Trans-Canada Highway

Grand Falls-Windsor

Twillingate

Gander

Terra Nova National Park

St. John's

Mt. Pearl

Conception Bay South

Witless Bay Bird Sanctuary

Placentia

Cape St. Mary's Bird Sanctuary

ISLAND OF NEWFOUNDLAND

10

NEWFOUNDLAND & LABRADOR Physical Map

Elevation

| 4000 | 3000 | 2000 | 1000 | 500 | 200 | 0 Meters |
| 13000 | 10000 | 6500 | 3300 | 1600 | 700 | 0 Feet |

—— Regional boundary
—·—·— International border

300 Kilometers
200 Miles

0   50   100   150   200
0   100   200

N
W   E
S

ATLANTIC OCEAN

Grand Banks

Labrador Current

Labrador Sea

Strait of Belle Isle

APPALACHIAN

Conception Bay
Cape Spear
Avalon Peninsula
Funk Island
Fogo Island
Gander River
Grand Lake
Long Range Mountains
St-Pierre & Miquelon (France)

SHIELD

Great Northern Peninsula

Humber River

Gulf of St. Lawrence

CANADIAN

Lake Melville

Smallwood Reservoir

Naskaupi River

Churchill River

QUÉBEC

Hudson Strait

Mt. Caubvick (5,420 ft./1,652 m)

Torngat Mts.

NOVA SCOTIA

PRINCE EDWARD ISLAND

NEW BRUNSWICK

Newfoundland and Labrador has two land regions—the Appalachian Region and the Canadian Shield. The Appalachian Region covers the entire island. The Long Range Mountains, part of the Appalachian Mountain system, rise in western Newfoundland. These mountains form the backbone of the island's Great Northern Peninsula. Surrounded by water on three sides, the **peninsula** juts northward to meet the Strait of Belle Isle.

Deep bays spattered with small islands cut up the northeastern coast of Newfoundland. Hundreds of fishing villages occupy the best coves (small,

On western Newfoundland, Gros Morne National Park is situated in the Long Range Mountains.

sheltered bays) and harbors on this shore, even though ice makes fishing impossible for much of the winter.

The Avalon Peninsula, on the island's southeastern corner, is the most heavily settled part of the province. The province's capital city, St. John's, is located here. Newfoundland's only other major city, Corner Brook, lies midway along the western coast.

Inland, the Appalachian Region becomes a rolling **plateau,** or highland. Forests and **peat bogs** (wetlands with large deposits of decaying plant matter) create a patchwork across the area.

The Canadian Shield spans much of northern Canada, including all of Labrador. A vast plateau, the shield is made up of ancient rock. In Labrador the rock holds rich mineral deposits, especially of iron ore.

St. John's is the province's biggest city.

13

Labrador is much bigger, much colder, much wilder, and much more isolated than Newfoundland. About 40 fishing villages dot Labrador's shore. The largest towns—Labrador City, Happy Valley–Goose Bay, Churchill Falls, and Wabush—lie inland.

Spruce forests, peat bogs, lakes, and high hills stretch across much of the interior. The soil is too poor and the growing season too short to earn a living from farming. But many Labradorians keep vegetable gardens and, in the southeast, raise a few dairy cows.

The Torngat Mountains contain the highest peak in eastern Canada.

Lake Melville, which is not actually a lake but a **fjord**, divides the eastern coast of Labrador. This deep arm of the sea extends far into the interior. Most of the Native people of Labrador live on the coast north of Lake Melville. Here, cliffs and mountains jut up from the edge of the sea. The Torngat Mountains, in the extreme north, feature Mount Caubvick. Rising 5,420 feet (1,652 meters), it is the highest peak in the entire province.

Labrador's major rivers, the Churchill and the Naskaupi, empty into Lake Melville. A series of **dikes** (barriers) built near Churchill Falls in western Labrador created the Smallwood Reservoir, the largest freshwater lake in the province. Water from the reservoir is used to turn motors that produce electricity. The Exploits, Humber, and

Few roads exist in Labrador. For transportation, many residents rely on ferryboats that travel along the coast.

Gander are chief rivers on the island of Newfoundland. Its largest lake is Grand Lake.

Two major ocean currents affect the province's climate. The currents act like rivers within the sea, carrying much more water than the biggest rivers on land. The Gulf Stream travels northward, bringing water from warm southern seas, while the Labrador Current sweeps down from the icy waters of the Arctic.

The waters of the Gulf Stream, which pass near Newfoundland, warm and moisten the air above the current. When this warm, damp air meets cold air, the combination produces fog. Thick mist often gathers over the southern coast of the island, which is famous for its dense fog.

The Labrador Current is another story. One branch of the current hugs the province's eastern shores. The current's waters are already so cold that a few weeks of bitter winter weather are enough to start freezing the surface of the ocean off the coast of Labrador. At first the cold forms a layer of slushy ice called slob. As it continues to freeze, the slob ice hardens into **ice floes,** or pancakes of ice, that drift south on the Labrador Current.

The Labrador Current carries another load, too—**icebergs**. These pieces of glaciers from Greenland and from the Arctic slowly creep into the sea. Many icebergs get caught in the swift Labrador Current. Strong northeasterly winds may drive some of these icebergs into shallow water. Stuck on a shoal, or underwater ridge of sand or rock, these gleaming mountains of blue-white ice may last for months.

Tourists love icebergs and shoot miles of film. Fishers, whose nets are often torn by drifting chunks of ice, see them differently.

17

Lichens are one of the few types of plants that thrive in the tundra region of Labrador.

The Labrador Current chills Labrador's coast all year. Summer temperatures average only 50° F (10° C) and winter temperatures only 1° F (–17° C). The climate in the Torngat Mountains and in Labrador's interior is even colder. Newfoundland is generally warmer than Labrador. Typical temperatures in St. John's are 24° F (–4° C) in the winter and 60° F (16° C) in the summer.

Every year about 60 inches (152 centimeters) of rain and 77 inches (196 cm) of snow fall on the island. Labrador gets much less rain, about 20 inches (51 cm) a year. But 170 inches (432 cm) of snow fall annually, most of it from December to March.

The melting of the snow and the icebergs is a sure sign of spring in the province. Wildflowers such as butterworts, goldthreads, and pitcher plants begin to bloom. In the **tundra** (treeless plain) of northern Labrador, only small plants such as mosses, lichens, and shrubs grow. Forests of spruce, balsam fir, and birch cover about 40 percent of the island and about 20 percent of Labrador.

Closely related to reindeer, caribou have broad hooves for walking on snow and on wet spongy ground.

Moose, caribou, lynx, mink, otters, red foxes, partridge, black bears, and snowshoe hare live on Newfoundland. Moose and hare were introduced to the island years ago as a source of food. Moose are so abundant nowadays that they are a major traffic hazard, appearing suddenly on highways at night.

Labrador has fewer moose and many more caribou than the island. In fact, the world's largest caribou herd roams Labrador during the calving season. Labrador is home to the same kinds of mammals as Newfoundland, as well as wolves, porcupines, and marten. Sea mammals such as seals, whales, porpoises, and dolphins swim along Labrador's coast.

Thousands of years ago, the Maritime Archaic Indians fashioned weapons for hunting and used tools to make clothing and shelter.

Cod is King

People have lived in Newfoundland and Labrador for at least 8,000 years. The first people, known as the Maritime Archaic Indians, were hunters. Many different groups of Native people have since lived in the region.

The Beothuk, who may have been descendants of the Maritime Archaic Indians, fished and hunted along the coastal waters of Newfoundland in bark canoes. The Dorset people occupied the coast of Labrador beginning about 500 B.C.

Dorset artists carved humans and other figures from soapstone.

21

Norse explorers led by Leif Eriksson sailed westward from Greenland about A.D. 1000. They landed on the rocky shores of Labrador and on the island of Newfoundland, where they may have spent the winter. Eriksson is the first European known to have explored part of North America.

In 1003 Thorfinn Karlsefni, another Norseman from Greenland, built the first European settlement in North America at L'Anse aux Meadows, on northern Newfoundland. The harsh climate and conflicts with the Native peoples caused the settlers to leave the island after just a few years. During

Leif Eriksson was probably the first European to set foot in Newfoundland. The explorer earned the nickname Leif the Lucky by saving shipwrecked sailors.

The Inuit of northern Labrador wore thick clothing made from caribou skins, which were sewn together with needles carved from the animals' antlers.

their short stay, Thorfinn's wife, Gudrid, gave birth to Snorri—the first European child known to be born in North America.

Within a few hundred years, bands of Inuit began moving into Labrador from farther north. These Native people fished for cod, salmon, and capelin along the coast. They also harpooned sea mammals, including seals, walrus, and whales. Hunting provided food and other necessities. The Inuit fashioned animal teeth and bones into tools, made oil from the fat, and sewed clothing from the furs and skins. Indians known as the Innu tracked caribou through the Labrador interior.

In 1497 John Cabot, an Italian explorer working for England, landed on Newfoundland. When Cabot returned to the British Isles, he and his crew reported that the schools of cod in the waters off Newfoundland were so thick that they slowed the ship.

John Cabot was amazed at the number of fish in the waters off the shores of Newfoundland.

Cabot's accounts excited the merchants of Europe, where cod was a popular food and the fishery, or fishing business, was important. Within a few years, the French, Portuguese, and Spanish were crossing the rough Atlantic Ocean to fish off the stormy coast of Newfoundland and Labrador for the summer.

Many captains stationed their fleets just southeast of the Avalon Peninsula. Called the Grand Banks, this shallow stretch of the Atlantic Ocean was the most productive cod-fishing region in the world.

The Spanish sent whaling ships as well. Whale oil, which was made from whale fat, was an important fuel in Europe. Hunters had killed so many whales that few of the giant sea mammals remained in European waters. Whalers who sailed to the rich shores of Labrador and Newfoundland harpooned enough whales to become wealthy in one voyage.

A Whale of a Gale

In the fall of 1565, a sudden gale capsized a Spanish galleon called the *San Juan* while it was moored in the Strait of Belle Isle, off the southeastern coast of Labrador. The captain and his crew were spared. But their summer's yield—about 55,000 gallons of whale oil (worth about $6 million nowadays)—was almost all lost.

More than 400 years later, in 1978, divers located the remains of the *San Juan*. It was the oldest ship ever to be discovered in Canadian waters. Historians now could recreate a day in the life of a Spanish whaler from the 1500s.

The whalers set sail for Newfoundland and Labrador every summer on large ships equipped with several smaller crafts called whaleboats. Each ship carried a crew of up to 2,000 people.

Some of the sailors were pages—teenage boys learning the trade for a small percentage of the profits. As the boys gained experience, they became full-fledged seamen and increased their earnings. To earn even more, some seamen mastered special skills, such as harpooning or navigating.

Harpooners left the main ship in a harbor and boarded the whaleboats to approach their target. Spanish hunters preferred to track what became known as the right whale, so-called because it swam slowly and floated when dead—making it the right, or easiest, whale to pursue. Once the whale had died, whalers towed it to the side of the harbored ship and stripped the animal of its valuable fat, or blubber, which was taken ashore and boiled into an oil.

The crew usually slept on the ship, but many of their duties took place on land. The sailors set up stations on shore, where they made wooden barrels to store the oil for the return trip.

Whaling expeditions were popular as a quick way to get rich. The *San Juan* crew may have worked for naught. But the shipwreck has helped connect Newfoundlanders and Labradorians to the past.

In 1583 explorer Sir Humphrey Gilbert, amid fishermen from all over Europe, boldly claimed the Avalon Peninsula and the rest of the island for England. No one questioned his claim, and fishermen from France, Spain, and Portugal continued to return summer after summer.

Early attempts by the British to build permanent, year-round settlements on the island met with little success. The wealthy fishing merchants

Soon after Humphrey Gilbert (standing center) *visited Newfoundland, a growing number of small British fisheries* (facing page) *began working year-round along the coasts of Newfoundland and Labrador.*

who sent ships to Newfoundland all summer were against having to share the waters with residents. The merchants encouraged fishermen to attack settlers. The harsh climate, poor soil for farming, and frequent raids by pirates also doomed several settlements.

Outports, or small fishing villages, got started anyway. Many early settlers were fishermen who feared they would be pressed into military service if they returned to Britain. To avoid being caught, some of them settled in coves that were difficult to reach.

The European settlers and seasonal fishermen changed the lives of the region's Native peoples. Europeans, who had guns, settled in the coastal hunting and fishing areas used by the Beothuk. Gradually, the Indians were pushed inland, where they were unable to thrive on what they could hunt. European diseases, such as tuberculosis, further weakened the Beothuk.

Other Native groups held on to their homelands and hunting grounds. By the early 1600s, the Micmac had settled far from Europeans on southwestern Newfoundland. In Labrador, Inuit people frequently clashed with European fishermen and seal hunters on the Strait of Belle Isle. But when the encounters became deadly, the Inuit moved farther north. The Innu worked with French fur traders and did not compete with anyone for fishing grounds. All of the Native groups, however, lost many people to European diseases.

The British and French eventually became the leading European fishers off the coasts of Newfoundland. In 1662 the French built Placentia, a fort on the southern coast of Newfoundland.

When the British king William III attacked France in 1689, the British and French in Newfoundland began to fight over fishing grounds. King William's War ended in 1713, and Britain gained control of the entire island. The French had to abandon Placentia but were allowed to continue fishing and drying their fish on the

northern and western shores of the island. This area became known as the French Shore.

In 1754 the British and French in North America began their final struggle for control of the continent. By 1756 the war had spread to Europe, where it was eventually known as the Seven Years' War. On Newfoundland the British drove the French off the French Shore, and the French briefly occupied St. John's, an important harbor on the Avalon Peninsula.

By the war's end in 1763, France had lost almost all its land in North America. But the British agreed to return the French Shore to the French and gave them the islands of Saint-Pierre and Miquelon just south of Newfoundland. These islands, which

A cartoon drawn in the 1700s shows British soldiers rounding up Newfoundlanders to fight the French in the Seven Years' War.

still belong to France, became a home for Frenchmen who fished off the coast of Newfoundland.

St. John's grew rapidly in the early 1800s.

From Fertile to Folding Fisheries

Although the British had claimed Newfoundland in the late 1500s, they had never officially made it a **colony.** Their main interest in the island had always been fish. Captains of fishing fleets took charge of local affairs during the fishing season, leaving Newfoundlanders without leadership during the winters.

By the early 1800s, the year-round population of Europeans on the island had crept up to 20,000. These settlers wanted a voice in local affairs and a stable government to enforce laws.

Most Inuit families lived in northern Labrador, where few Europeans settled.

As the British gained control on Newfoundland, the Beothuk disappeared. British attacks, deadly diseases, and the loss of fishing and hunting grounds caused the Beothuk to die out. Fur traders captured Demasduwit *(above)* in 1818. When her husband, chief Nonos-a-ba-sut, tried to rescue her, he was killed. By 1820 she had died of tuberculosis. The loss of Nonos-a-ba-sut left the Beothuk leaderless.

In 1824 Britain recognized the island of Newfoundland and the coast of Labrador as a colony. Eight years later, British authorities gave the colonists some control over their government by allowing them to elect Newfoundlanders into office. But the British government still had to approve any laws passed by these local leaders. Finally, in 1855, Britain gave Newfoundland and Labrador the power to control its local affairs without British approval, a form of leadership called **responsible government**.

Even with local self-government, life was difficult in the colony. Most families in the outports rarely made enough money to pay cash for the food and clothes they needed for winter. Instead, they bought their supplies on credit, eventually paying the merchants with fish. Under these arrangements, families had to turn over their fish at low prices to the merchants. This practice kept entire communities poor.

A FISHY BUSINESS

For hundreds of years in Newfoundland, fish meant cod. Cod was the most important fish because of its abundance and its popularity in Europe. Without cod, Newfoundland would never have become a colony.

In the outports, the fishery was a family business. A family's entire income depended on the fishery, so children took on heavy chores as soon as they were able. Men and boys age 13 and over did most of the fishing. Women and children did much of the work that followed, and there was lots of it.

Nearly all the fish had to be cured with salt to keep the catch from spoiling. This process began as soon as the cod was landed. First the fish had to be gutted, headed, and split—the organs, heads, and backbones had to be removed. The fish were then piled in layers and buried in salt for a few days.

Afterward, family members spread the catch on platforms called flakes, where it dried in the open air for many days. To keep rain and dampness from spoiling the fish, children carried the cod into shelter every night and whenever the sky threatened rain.

By the mid-1800s, saltfish production in Newfoundland was topping 1 million pounds (450,000 kilograms) a year. But the price paid for the fish kept changing, depending on what Europeans were willing to pay. When prices were low, families made little or no profit, no matter how hard they worked.

33

In 1866 a telegraph cable reached the Newfoundland coast, allowing the first direct communication between British North America and Europe. Workers, operating from a steamship, had laid the cable under the ocean floor.

St. John's, however, boomed. Nearly all the goods bought and sold by the colony's 1,600 villages passed through St. John's harbor. Seagoing ships delivered salt, molasses, flour, fishing gear, and household items. The ships left with goods from the outports—fish, cod-liver oil, sealskins, and seal oil. This bustling trade brought wealth to the merchants of St. John's.

As fishermen occupied the best sites along the shores of Newfoundland, newcomers began settling in Labrador. The fishing season was shorter there because of the cold climate, but fish, seals, and fur-bearing animals such as foxes and mink were abundant.

Many Labradorian settlers married Inuit women. The two groups learned from each other. The Inuit began using

manufactured goods from Europe—especially rifles, steel knives, and steel traps. From the Inuit, many whites learned to hunt seals and caribou, to travel by dogsled, and to make sealskin boots for winter.

For the most part, the colonial government of Newfoundland, located in St. John's, neglected Labrador. Officials, for example, collected taxes from Labradorians but never bothered making arrangements for them to vote.

Newfoundlanders were busy developing new industries, especially mining and forestry, to strengthen their economy. Copper and iron ore were discovered on Newfoundland in the late 1800s. To reach the mines and forests of the interior, Newfoundlanders built a railway across the island beginning in 1882.

Wilfred Grenfell—a doctor and Christian missionary—arrived in the colony in 1892. He toured the coasts of Newfoundland and Labrador and treated hundreds of patients. He also raised money to build hospitals, nursing stations, and an orphanage in isolated areas where people had little or no health care.

35

When World War I broke out in 1914, thousands of young Newfoundlanders and Labradorians joined the army. More than 1,000 young men of the Newfoundland Regiment lost their lives.

Soldiers at Pleasantville practice shooting machine guns as they ready for World War I.

In 1929 the economies of countries around the world fell apart. For the following 10 years—during a period known as the Great Depression, or Hungry Thirties—banks and factories closed. On Newfoundland, thousands of workers were out of work.

In 1934 leaders in St. John's asked Britain for financial help. Britain appointed seven men, together known as the Commission of Government, to govern Newfoundland and Labrador and to review its debts. Newfoundlanders and Labradorians had abandoned responsible government, but they had little choice.

The beginning of another war, World War II (1939–1945), helped Newfoundland and Labrador recover from the Depression. Its location far out in the Atlantic Ocean offered ideal

sites for launching military ships and aircraft to Europe.

During the war, Canada and the United States constructed several military bases in Newfoundland and Labrador. The Royal Canadian Air Force station at Goose Bay began operations in 1942. These and other wartime projects gave thousands of Newfoundlanders and Labradorians their first well-paid jobs.

When the war ended, Newfoundland and Labrador's economy had improved, but the people faced a difficult decision. They could remain dependent on Britain, return to responsible government, or join the larger and stronger country of Canada. Joseph R. Smallwood, a former journalist, led the campaign to unite Newfoundland and Labrador with Canada.

After a series of furious debates and close votes, Newfoundland and Labrador chose to become the 10th province of Canada. **Confederation,** or admission to the Dominion of Canada, took place in 1949. Smallwood became the province's first premier, or leader.

In the 1950s, companies began mining huge deposits of iron ore near Labrador's border with Québec. The companies built towns for the miners and a railway to haul the ore south to the Gulf of Saint Lawrence. From there, ships brought much of the mineral to steel mills in the United States.

In the 1960s, workers began building one of the largest hydropower projects in the world at Churchill Falls in Labrador. The underground powerhouse now supplies electricity to Labrador, Québec, and the United States.

Despite these developments, Newfoundland and Labrador still relied mostly on fish for income. But by the 1970s, cod was a resource in trouble. Fishermen from other countries had begun to use boats called trawlers, which were equipped to fish year-round, even in winter among the floes of Labrador and northern Newfoundland. These fleets were taking more than 800,000 tons (725,760 metric tons) of cod a year—more than three times as much as the fishermen took when they only worked the summers.

Year-round fishing by foreign trawlers threatened to wipe out cod. The catches of local fishermen fell to disastrous levels. In 1977, to give cod and other fish a chance to grow and to reproduce, Canada began setting limits on how many fish could be harvested

within 200 miles (322 km) of its coast. This greatly reduced the catch of the trawlers and helped prevent fish stocks from dwindling.

ince built fleets of trawlers to land huge catches year-round, as other countries had done not long before.

By the late 1980s, fish stocks had again dropped to dangerously low levels. Most people blamed overfishing. But a recent drop in ocean temperatures, which makes it harder for young fish to live and grow, and an increase in the fish-eating seal population may also have contributed to the decline.

In 1992 the Canadian government banned the fishing of northern cod—Newfoundland and Labrador's most important stock off its Atlantic coast. In 1994 the ban was extended to all cod fishing, leaving thousands of Newfoundlanders and Labradorians jobless. Many people are now struggling to find new ways to make money in a province that was built on fishing.

Hundreds of Newfoundlanders and Labradorians who had given up on fishing now flocked back to it. In addition, large fish companies in the prov-

Life after Cod

For 400 years, cod alone was enough to attract thousands of people to Newfoundland and Labrador. But as the province has grown, so has its need to branch into other industries.

Industries based on other natural resources, such as minerals and forests, make up a good portion of the province's economy. But many experts agree that, like fish, other natural resources cannot employ Newfoundlanders and Labradorians forever. So the province is trying to expand its service industry and its high-tech manufacturing.

In the early 1990s, just before the fishery collapsed, about 25,000 fishers (6 percent of the workforce) lived in the province. Another 26,000 people processed the catch at the fish plants. Now most of these people are out of work. The Canadian government has set up programs so that unemployed fishers and plant workers can learn new skills to use in other jobs.

Primary industries that depend on Newfoundland and Labrador's trees (below) *and minerals such as iron ore* (left) *help support the province's economy.*

41

The hundreds of small coastal villages in the province, however, offer little chance of other work. Without fish, many of these places have no reason to exist. To find work, some people are moving to other parts of Canada. They hope to return when cod fishing is permitted once again.

Empty, weathered boats sit on a dock.

The Wave of the Future

"Move on down the line!" yelled Jim to his partner as they struggled to pack the mesh socks with spat. Mussel spat is the seed from which shellfish called mussels grow. Mussels *(inset)* are one of a handful of types of water life Newfoundlanders and Labradorians are beginning to harvest on fish farms.

Fish farming is also called aquaculture—the raising of fish, shellfish, or seaweed in a controlled environment. By regulating food, breeding, and water conditions, an aquaculturist can produce large numbers of healthy water life in a short period of time. Many of Newfoundland and Labrador's bays and coves are perfect for aquaculture because they are sheltered from harsh Atlantic storms.

Currently, aquaculturists in the province raise cod, rainbow trout, steelhead, Atlantic salmon, Arctic char, mussels, and scallops. The fish are kept in tanks or in mesh pens set in coastal waters. Tiny holes in the mesh allow a constant flushing of seawater, so the water in the pen remains fresh and stocked with nutrients. To help the fish grow, aquaculturists feed them a high-protein diet.

Fish farming can be difficult. Mistakes can cost thousands of dollars. Aquaculturists have to learn how to take care of their stocks through harsh winters, when ice covers the water. Disease and wildlife can damage fish stocks. And in some cases, aquaculturists must wait several years for their fish to become big enough to sell.

Even with these risks, aquaculture offers hope for the fishery in Newfoundland and Labrador. While many Newfoundlanders and Labradorians wait for the day when cod and other fish will once again fill coastal waters, some residents prefer to grow their own. Mussels, anyone?

Some Newfoundlanders and Labradorians rely on the province's other natural resources for jobs. Although soil has never been rich or plentiful in Labrador or on the island, 1 percent of the province's workers are farmers. Vegetables, especially potatoes, are grown mainly on western Newfoundland. Farmers near St. John's and Corner Brook raise mostly dairy cattle and chickens.

More than half of Newfoundland and Labrador is covered with trees. Spruce and fir are the most abundant, but birch is also common. About 1 percent of the province's workers have jobs in forestry.

Because of the province's long, harsh winters, trees in the region rarely grow thick or tall. But loggers fell spruce and fir for making high quality newsprint. Other trees are cut into two-by-fours. Plywood and large-sized lumber must be shipped to Newfoundland and Labrador from other provinces.

Girls pick strawberries at a farm about 40 miles (65 kilometers) northeast of Corner Brook.

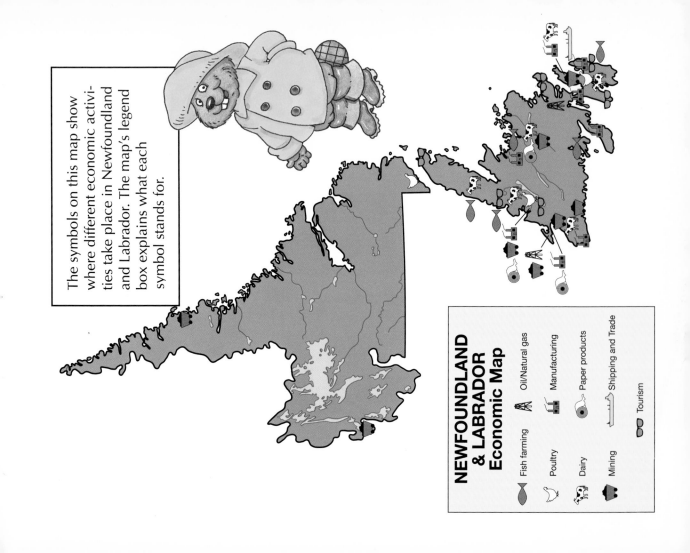

The symbols on this map show where different economic activities take place in Newfoundland and Labrador. The map's legend box explains what each symbol stands for.

NEWFOUNDLAND & LABRADOR Economic Map

Fish farming
Poultry
Dairy
Mining

Oil/Natural gas
Manufacturing
Paper products
Shipping and Trade

Tourism

A ship outfitted with a rig for drilling offshore oil rests in St. John's harbor.

Mining employs only about 2 percent of the province's workforce but brings in a lot of money. About 80 percent of the money earned from mining comes from iron ore, all of which is taken from two large mines in Labrador. The mainland also yields marble and several semiprecious stones, including labradorite and garnet. Miners extract gold near Port aux Basques, on southwestern Newfoundland. Other minerals on the island include zinc and limestone.

In the 1970s, major oil deposits were found under the Grand Banks at a site called Hibernia. But getting the oil from this stormy part of the Atlantic Ocean, in the path of drifting icebergs, will be a difficult and expensive job. Workers are building a huge, concrete platform to support the heavy equipment needed to pump oil from the ocean floor into tankers. These large ships can then carry the oil to refineries, where it will be processed into gasoline and other oil products.

Oil drilling is scheduled to begin in the late 1990s, but many Newfoundlanders and Labradorians worry about the risk of a large oil spill. Some people believe accidents are certain to happen, especially in winter when the sea turns fierce. Oil spilled into the ocean could further spoil the province's fishing grounds. Despite the risks, the province needs jobs so badly that most people are anxious for drilling to begin.

Some fish and shellfish are still processed at plants in Newfoundland and Labrador.

In the early 1990s, about 10 percent of the province's workforce was employed in manufacturing. Most people worked in fish plants, where they cut cod into fillets. The ban on cod fishing, however, has shut down many plants, reducing the number of people employed in manufacturing.

But Newfoundland still has a strong manufacturing industry. Products made on the island include ice cream, beer, margarine, boots, furniture, and electrical instruments.

Newfoundland's forests provide timber for three pulp mills, but just barely. Logs are shipped to the island's mills, where workers grind the wood into pulp for making paper. To help replace some of the old forest, foresters plant new trees every year. But with three pulp mills using the island's wood, some people worry that the forests won't grow back quickly enough to replace the trees loggers are cutting down.

The number of jobs in Newfoundland's paper and logging industries has been declining as machines do more of the work people once did.

Dockworkers unload supplies at an outport that can be reached only by boat.

Most of the province's workforce—about three-fourths—have service jobs. Service workers help other people or businesses. Some service workers are teachers, doctors, or government employees. Shipping and trade employ many of the province's service workers.

Newfoundlanders and Labradorians are finding more jobs in tourism, a growing service industry. Guides, hotel clerks, and others assist tourists from all over the world. Visitors are drawn to the province's spectacular rocky coasts, historical sites, and charming villages. Tourists in Newfoundland and Labrador also discover a friendly, isolated place—a place where the people have learned to live with the forces of nature.

Tourists and residents alike enjoy the province's rugged wilderness.

Tradition Lives On

Nearly everyone in the province of Newfoundland and Labrador grows up with the smell of salt in the air and the sound of waves crashing against a rocky shore. In Labrador dozens of small fishing villages line the rugged coast. On the island there are hundreds of them. No cities exist in Labrador and only a couple have been developed on the island. Nearly half of the province's 568,000 people live in villages or small towns with fewer than 5,000 people.

About 90 percent of Newfoundlanders and Labradorians have ancestors from the British Isles—England, Ireland, Wales, and Scotland. People with French roots make up less than 3 percent of the province's population. But on the Port au Port Peninsula, along the western coast of Newfoundland, people of French background are the majority.

Native people make up less than 1 percent of the province's total population. Many Micmac Indians live on the island of Newfoundland. Most of the Inuit and the Innu live in northern Labrador, where they outnumber people of European ancestry.

Many Labradorians are Inuit or Innu. On Newfoundland, most people are descended from Europeans.

When Europeans began settling in Newfoundland and Labrador, they brought the customs and tongues of their homelands with them. Long after certain words and habits of speech died out in the British Isles, Newfoundlanders and Labradorians—isolated from these changes—kept the old words and patterns alive.

Many of the Native communities in Labrador have also preserved their traditions and languages. The Okalakatiget Society broadcasts the news on radio and television in Inuktitut, the Inuit language. The Innu hire planes to take their families into the wilderness for months at a time to camp, hunt, and fish as their ancestors did.

Newfoundland English

Visitors to Newfoundland and Labrador are often confused by some curious habits of speech. They have trouble understanding Newfoundlanders.

For instance, a visiting doctor would be puzzled if a patient complained, "I got a clink in me tinker and I cain't glutch." (I have a swelling in my throat and I can't swallow.) Or, instead of saying, "Stay where you are until I get there," local residents say, "Stay where you're to, till I come where you're at."

The language is English—but with its own expressions, accents, and rules of grammar. Newfoundlanders take delight in their language. They have strong traces of the same accents their European ancestors brought from the British Isles. Many of the words have simply fallen out of use in other English-speaking countries. *Quintal,* for instance, is an old English measure for 112 pounds (51 kilograms) of fish.

Other words were probably invented in Newfoundland. For example, *ballicatter* describes the fringe of ice along the shore in winter. Accents and expressions vary so much from one local region to the next that Newfoundlanders can often tell where their neighbors come from by the way they speak.

In the summer, many areas of Labrador can be reached only by float plane (above), *which can take off and land on water. Since 1992, when the Trans Labrador Highway* (top) *opened, people have had an easier time traveling to parts of the Labrador interior. In winter Labradorians depend on snowmobiles* (right) *to get around.*

In Labrador, towns along the southern coast and the largest inland towns are connected by roads. To the north, residents rely on coastal boats in summer and planes in winter to carry passengers and freight.

Nearly every family in Labrador owns a snowmobile. This is how most people get around in winter. In the remote parts of the province, winter actually makes travel easier. All the lakes, rivers, and peat bogs make overland travel difficult in summer, but they are suddenly passable when they freeze over. In Labrador and on western Newfoundland, high hills, deep snow, and long winters make for excellent skiing.

Many vacationers come to Newfoundland to see the striking scenery. Two national parks—Gros Morne and Terra Nova—offer wildlife and majestic fjords. Visitors can also cruise the ocean to watch for whales and icebergs.

Sanctuaries at Witless Bay and Cape Saint Mary's protect birds, such as gannets and puffins, from egg hunters. Visitors can see millions of birds every spring during the nesting season.

L'Anse aux Meadows National Historic Site on the northern tip of the island is the location of the first Norse settlement in North America. Restorers have rebuilt Norse houses at the site to look as they did nearly 1,000 years ago.

Throughout Newfoundland and Labrador, several dozen summer festivals highlight the traditions of the people. Life in the outports is saluted at the Fish, Fun, and Folk Festival in Twillingate. At Point Amour, Labradorians sing, dance, and eat berries at the Bakeapple Folk Festival.

Traditional music takes center stage at some events, including the Newfoundland and Labrador Folk Festival in St. John's and the Brimstone Head Folk Festival on Fogo Island. Theater in the province is just as lively, especially in larger cities such as St. John's. The Resource Center for the Arts features various theater groups. Codco and the Rising Tide Theatre head the list of comedy groups in the province.

Newfoundlanders and Labradorians take pride in their strong and distinct

communities. The people appreciate their unique traditions and celebrate them through language, festivals, theater, and daily life.

Famous Newfoundlanders and Labradorians

Agnes Marion Ayre (1890–1940), from St. John's, was a gardener and painter who taught herself botany by collecting and drawing wildflowers. She illustrated several books, including *Wild Flowers of Newfoundland and Labrador,* and helped compile material for *Gray's Manual of Botany.*

2 **Robert Bartlett** (1875–1946) grew up hunting seals in icy water near his hometown of Brigus, Newfoundland. From this experience, he became an expert at navigating ships through ice-choked seas. At 22 he made his first of three trips to the North Pole with the explorer Robert Peary. Between 1926 and 1945, he led 19 expeditions to the Arctic.

Emile Benoit (1913–1992) is best-known as a self-taught violinist and composer of traditional folk music. Throughout Canada and the United States, the performer from L'Anse-a-Canards, Newfoundland, entertained audiences with lively stories to accompany his fiddle playing. A strong influence on younger musicians, Benoit helped revive an interest in Newfoundland's traditional music.

4 **Cassie Brown** (1916–1986), an author from Rose Blanche, Newfoundland, wrote about shipwrecks and seal fishing. Her best-known book is *Death on the Ice: The Newfoundland Sealing Disaster of 1914.*

■ **Johnny Burke** (1851–1930) wrote poems, songs, and musicals about his hometown of St. John's. Among his most famous songs are *Cod Liver Oil, The Trinity Cake,* and *Kelligrews Soiree.*

6 Craig Dobbin (born 1935), from Grand Bank, Newfoundland, is the founder and chairman of Canadian Helicopter Corporation (CHC), the world's largest helicopter company. CHC has more than 270 helicopters operating in over 15 countries.

■ **Julia Salter Earle** (1877–1945), from St. John's, was famous for helping poor people in Newfoundland. She learned about law from her job as a clerk, copying bills to be signed into law. With this knowledge she helped people in trouble gain their legal rights. She also helped women win the right to vote.

8 Mina Hubbard (1870–1953), born in Bewdley, Ontario, was the first white woman to explore central Labrador. Hubbard drew the first accurate map of the Naskaupi and George river systems. She wrote about her trip in the book *A Woman's Way Through Unknown Labrador.*

9 Percy Janes (born 1922), an award-winning author from St. John's, writes poems, short stories, and novels. Among his works are *House of Hate, Newfoundlanders,* and *No Cage for Conquerors.*

10 Marilyn John (born 1951) is a Micmac from the Conne River Reservation in Bay d'Espoir, Newfoundland. A tribal leader, John works to gain Indians more control over their land, education, medical care, and other concerns. In 1984 she helped 580 Micmac become officially recognized as Indians. By improving life for Native peoples, John believes their culture will thrive.

61

11 Karl Kenny (born 1960) made himself a millionaire in his 20s by starting a computer-components firm. In 1989 Kenny founded Matrix Technologies, Inc., in his hometown of St. John's. The company makes digital imaging systems and navigation computers for ships.

12 Kevin Major (born 1949) grew up in Stephenville and planned to become a doctor. But after college he decided to pursue a writing career. His books *Hold Fast* and *Far from Shore* feature teenagers as their main characters and have won awards for young adult fiction.

13 Greg Malone (born 1948), an actor from St. John's, helped form the theater group Codco in 1972. In *Cod on a Stick* and other shows, Codco pokes fun at a variety of people and situations. In the 1980s, the group began producing comedy for television and won several Gemini Awards. Malone is known for his imitation of President Ronald Reagan.

■ Joan Morrissey (1935–1978) began her musical career in 1959 as a country-music singer and quickly gained popularity. From nightclubs to main-stage musicals, the St. John's native was comfortable singing in a variety of musical styles. Morrisey recorded three albums, including *Live at the Admiral's Keg.*

■ Peter Penashue (born 1964) is from Sheshatshiu, Labrador. President of the Innu Nation since 1990, Penashue works to increase the rights of the Innu and improve their living conditions. He encourages nonviolent action against projects that threaten the Innu way of life.

16 Vera Perlin (1902–1974) championed the abilities of the mentally retarded and in 1955 founded the Newfoundland Association for the Help of Retarded Children. The experimental school was a success. By 1974, 10 schools had opened to teach basic job skills. In 1968 Perlin was named an officer of the Order of Canada.

17 Gordon Edward Pinsent (born 1930) is a writer and an award-winning actor from Grand Falls, Labrador. He both wrote and starred in the films *The Rowdyman* and *John and the Missus*. Pinsent can also be seen on television as Hap Shaughnessy in *The Red Green Show*.

■ **John Christopher Pratt** (born 1935), an artist, is known for landscapes and portraits that capture a harsh beauty and feeling of aloneness. Born in St. John's, Pratt is considered one of the greatest of contemporary Canadian painters.

19 Shanawdithit (1801–1829) was considered to be the last Beothuk. She was captured by British settlers on Newfoundland in 1823 and eventually was brought to St. John's, where she recorded the ways of her people in drawings and in stories.

20 Joseph Smallwood (1900–1991), from Gambo, Newfoundland, used his popularity as a radio broadcaster to convince Newfoundlanders to join the Dominion of Canada. In 1949 he became Newfoundland and Labrador's first premier, a post he held until 1972. In 1986 he was made Companion of the Order of Canada. Smallwood edited a four-volume work entitled *The Encyclopedia of Newfoundland and Labrador*.

21 Georgina Stirling (1867–1935), from Twillingate, Newfoundland, was an opera singer who toured throughout Canada, the United States, and Europe. She took the stage name Marie Toulinguet and became very popular in Italy, where she sang for the Italian royal family.

22 Shannon Tweed (born 1956) started her career as a model and then turned to acting, appearing on *Falcon Crest* for a season and on the daytime soap opera *Days of Our Lives* for two years. She has also starred in several movies, including *No Contest*. Tweed grew up in Whitbourne, Newfoundland.

63

Fast Facts

Provincial Symbols

Motto: *Quaerite Prime Fegnum Dei*
(Seek ye first the kingdom of God)
Nickname: the Rock
Flower: pitcher plant
Tree: black spruce
Bird: Atlantic puffin
Tartan: green for pine-clad hills, gold for sunlight, white
for snow, brown for iron ore, and red for the royal
standard of its ancestors

Provincial Highlights

Landmarks: Cabot Tower in St. John's, L'Anse aux
Meadows National Historic Site north of St. Anthony,
Cape Spear Lighthouse south of St. John's, Newfoundland
Museum in St. John's, Nain Museum in Nain, Red Bay
whaling site, Hebron Mission National Historic Site
in Hebron

Annual events: Winter Carnival throughout the
province (Jan.–March), Newfoundland and Labrador
Drama Festival in St. John's (April), Killigrew's Soiree in
Conception Bay (July), Labrador Canoe Regatta in
Happy Valley–Goose Bay (Aug.), St. John's Regatta (Aug.)

Population

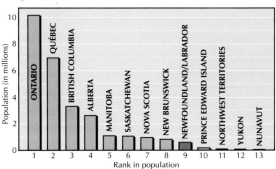

Population*: 568,000
Rank in population, nationwide: 9th
Population distribution: 54 percent urban; 46 percent
rural
Population density: 4 people per sq mi (1.5 per sq km)
Capital: St. John's (102,000*)
Major cities and towns (and populations*): Mount
Pearl (23,689), Corner Brook (22,410), Conception Bay
South (17,590), Grand Falls–Windsor (14,693), Gander
(10,339), Labrador City (9,061), Happy Valley–Goose
Bay (8,610)
Major ethnic groups*: British, 79 percent; multiple
backgrounds, 18 percent; French 2 percent; Indian,
Inuit, Métis, 1 percent

*1991 census

64

Endangered Species

Mammals: wolverine
Birds: harlequin duck, anatum peregrine falcon, piping plover
Reptiles: leatherback turtle

Geographic Highlights

Area (land/water): 156,648 sq mi (405,720 sq km)
Rank in area, nationwide: 10th
Highest point: Mt. Caubvick (5,420 ft/1,652 m)
Major lakes and rivers: Smallwood Reservoir, Lake Melville, Grand Lake, Churchill River, Exploits River, Humber River, Gander River

Economy

Percentage of Workers Per Job Sector

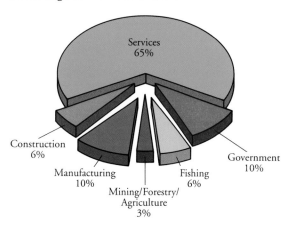

Services 65%
Construction 6%
Manufacturing 10%
Mining/Forestry/Agriculture 3%
Fishing 6%
Government 10%

Natural resources: forests, ocean fishing grounds, iron ore, zinc, limestone, semiprecious stones, fluorspar, gold, oil, natural gas
Agricultural products: chickens, eggs, milk, cattle, hogs, potatoes, turnips, carrots, broccoli, berries
Manufactured goods: fish products, paper products, boats, concrete, lumber, printed materials, roofing slate, floor tiles, flagstone, windows, footwear, gloves, high-tech equipment, ice cream, furniture

Energy

Electric power: hydroelectric power (95 percent), oil burning plants (5 percent)

65

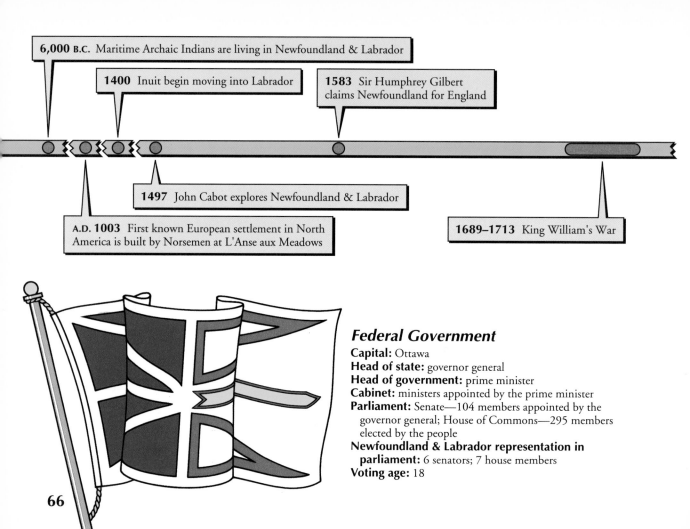

6,000 B.C. Maritime Archaic Indians are living in Newfoundland & Labrador

1400 Inuit begin moving into Labrador

1583 Sir Humphrey Gilbert claims Newfoundland for England

1497 John Cabot explores Newfoundland & Labrador

A.D. 1003 First known European settlement in North America is built by Norsemen at L'Anse aux Meadows

1689–1713 King William's War

Federal Government

Capital: Ottawa
Head of state: governor general
Head of government: prime minister
Cabinet: ministers appointed by the prime minister
Parliament: Senate—104 members appointed by the governor general; House of Commons—295 members elected by the people
Newfoundland & Labrador representation in parliament: 6 senators; 7 house members
Voting age: 18

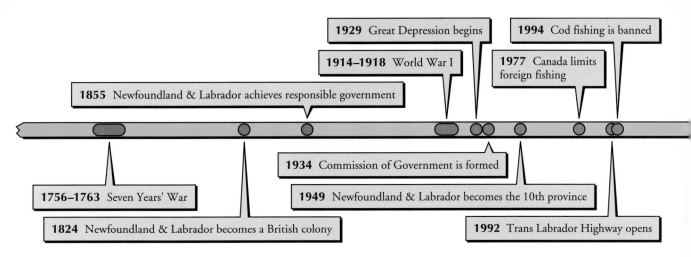

1929 Great Depression begins

1994 Cod fishing is banned

1914–1918 World War I

1977 Canada limits foreign fishing

1855 Newfoundland & Labrador achieves responsible government

1934 Commission of Government is formed

1756–1763 Seven Years' War

1949 Newfoundland & Labrador becomes the 10th province

1824 Newfoundland & Labrador becomes a British colony

1992 Trans Labrador Highway opens

Provincial Government

Capital: St. John's
Head of state: lieutenant governor
Head of government: premier
Cabinet: minsters appointed by the premier
Legislative Assembly: 52 members elected to terms that can last up to five years
Voting age: 18
Major political parties: Liberal, Progressive Conservative

Government Services

To help pay the people who work for Newfoundland and Labrador's government, residents pay taxes on money they earn and on many of the items they buy. The services run by the provincial government help assure Newfoundlanders and Labradorians of a high quality of life. Government funds pay for medical care, for education, for road building and repairs, and for other facilities such as libraries and parks. In addition, the government has funds to help people who are disabled, elderly, or poor.

Glossary

colony   A territory ruled by a country some distance away.

Confederation   Initially, under the British North America Act of 1867, the union of four British colonies to form the Dominion of Canada. The union gradually expanded as other colonies joined the dominion.

dike   A barrier constructed to stop the sea, a river, or a lake from flooding low land.

fjord   A long, narrow, steep-sided inlet into the seacoast.

ice floe   A thick, flat piece of floating ice.

glacier   A large body of ice and snow that moves slowly over land.

iceberg   A piece of ice that has broken off from a glacier and is floating in the sea. In some cases, only a small part of the iceberg can be seen above the ocean's surface.

outport   A small fishing village, especially on Newfoundland. Outport is also used to describe a country's secondary ports.

peat bog   Wet, spongy ground rich in decaying plant matter (peat), which is sometimes dried for use as fuel.

peninsula   A stretch of land almost completely surrounded by water.

plateau   A large, relatively flat area that stands above the surrounding land.

responsible government   A form of government that made the British-appointed governor answerable to an assembly elected by the people. Responsible government gave colonists control over local affairs.

tundra   A treeless plain found in arctic and subarctic regions. The ground beneath the top layer of soil is permanently frozen, but the topsoil thaws for a short period each summer, allowing mosses, lichens, and dwarf shrubs to grow.

Pronunciation Guide

Appalachian (ap-uh-LAY-chuhn)

Belle Isle (behl EYE-uhl)

Beothuk (BAY-uh-thuk)

Eriksson, Leif (EHR-ihks-suhn, LAYF)

Gros Morne (grohs MAWRN)

Inuit (EE-noo-eet)

L'Anse aux Meadows (LANS oh MEH-dohs)

Naskaupi (nuh-SKAH-pee)

Newfoundland (NEW-fuhnd-LAND)

Nova Scotia (noh-vuh SKOH-shuh)

Nunavut (NU-nah-voot)

Québec (kay-behk)

Torngat (TAWRN-gat)

Index

About the Author

Lawrence Jackson, a native of southern Alberta, has spent 18 years in Labrador and has lived on Newfoundland since 1990. He has worked as a reporter, an adult educator, a prospector, and a freelance writer. His work has appeared in most major Canadian magazines. *Newfoundland & Labrador* is his first children's book. Jackson lives with his wife and three children in St. John's.

Acknowledgments

Ned Therrien, pp. 2, 8, 49 (right), 50, 54 (right), 59 (left); Terry Boles, pp. 6, 10, 45, 65; Cindy Kilgore Brown, pp. 7, 19; Betty Groskin, pp. 8 (inset), 52 (inset), 69; Mapping Specialists, Ltd., pp. 10–11, 45; Steve Warble/Mountain Magic, pp. 12, 46–47, 52; Norma Watts, pp. 13, 59 (upper right), 71; Michael Hockney, pp. 14, 18, 41 (both), 51, 56 (top & lower left); Industry, Science & Technology Canada Photo, pp. 15, 54 (left); © Rob Simpson, p. 17; Keith Nicol Photo, pp. 20, 44; Collection of the Newfoundland Museum, pp. 21, 29; Confederation Life Gallery of Canadian History, pp. 22, 26, 34; National Archives of Canada, pp. 23 (C–95201), 27 (C–70648), 30 (C–41605), 32 (C–87698), 60 (right, C–25962), 63 (top left, C–38862); Library of Congress, pp. 24, 33 (lower left), 35; Peabody Museum, Harvard University, p. 31 (N26859); Laura Westlund, pp. 33 (upper right), 64, 65 (right), 66–67; Provincial Archives of Newfoundland & Labrador, pp. 36 (B5–180), 63 (middle right); Government of Newfoundland & Labrador, Dept. of Fisheries, Food & Agriculture, pp. 38–39, 48; Lucille Sukalo, pp. 42, 58; Clifford Grinling/Enterprise Newfoundland & Labrador, p. 43; Government of Newfoundland & Labrador, Dept. of Industry, Trade & Technology, p. 49 (left); Hubert Best, p. 56 (lower right); Rosanna White/St. John's Folk Arts Council, p. 59 (lower right); Tootin's, p. 60 (left); CHC Helicopter Corporation, p. 61 (top); Harry Cuff Publications, p. 61 (left); Centre for Newfoundland Studies, Memorial University of Newfoundland, pp. 61 (middle), 62 (middle, bottom), 63 (top right, bottom left); Marilyn John/Conne River Indian Band, p. 61 (lower right); Matrix Technologies, p. 62 (top left); Ned Pratt, p. 62 (top right)